What's the Issue?

WHAT'S DIVERSITY?

By David Anthony

Published in 2019 by
KidHaven Publishing, an Imprint of Greenhaven Publishing, LLC
353 3rd Avenue
Suite 255
New York, NY 10010

Designer: Andrea Davison-Bartolotta
Editor: Katie Kawa

Photo credits: Cover (bottom), p. 15 (main) Hero Images/Getty Images; cover (top) Sheila Fitzgerald/Shutterstock.com; p. 4 Umberto Shtanzman/Shutterstock.com; p. 5 Dirk Anschutz/Stone/ Getty Images; p. 7 kup1984/iStock/Thinkstock; p. 8 Roberto Gerometta/Lonely Planet Images/Getty Images; p. 9 Jeenah Moon/Bloomberg via Getty Images; p. 11 glenda/Shutterstock.com; p. 13 GaudiLab/Shutterstock.com; p. 15 (inset) FatCamera/E+/Getty Images; p. 17 Ira L. Black/Corbis via Getty Images; p. 18 Kathy Hutchins/Shutterstock.com; p. 19 Ian West/PA Images via Getty Images; p. 21 Creativika Graphics/Shutterstock.com.

Library of Congress Cataloging-in-Publication Data

Names: Anthony, David, 1971- author.
Title: What's diversity? / David Anthony.
Description: New York : KidHaven Publishing, [2019] | Series: What's the issue? | Includes index.
Identifiers: LCCN 2018019057 (print) | LCCN 2018021168 (ebook) | ISBN 9781534528031 (eBook) | ISBN 9781534528024 (library bound book) | ISBN 9781534528000 (pbk. book) | ISBN 9781534528017 (6 pack)
Subjects: LCSH: Cultural pluralism–Juvenile literature. | Multiculturalism–Juvenile literature.
Classification: LCC HM1271 (ebook) | LCC HM1271 .A578 2019 (print) | DDC 305.8–dc23
LC record available at https://lccn.loc.gov/2018019057

Printed in the United States of America

CPSIA compliance information: Batch #BW19KL: For further information contact Greenhaven Publishing LLC, New York, New York at 1-844-317-7404.

Please visit our website, www.greenhavenpublishing.com. For a free color catalog of all our high-quality books, call toll free 1-844-317-7404 or fax 1-844-317-7405.

CONTENTS

Something to Celebrate

Imagine a world where everyone is the same. It wouldn't look anything like the world we live in, and it would be a very boring place! No two people on Earth are exactly alike, and our differences make us special.

When we celebrate the fact that the world is made up of many different kinds of people, we're celebrating diversity. However, some people wish everyone looked, acted, and thought the same. These people are afraid of diversity, but most people know it's not a bad thing to be different. Diversity is an important part of our communities, our country, and our world.

Facing the Facts 🔍

The World Bank has stated that there are around 7.5 billion people living on Earth.

4

How can you celebrate diversity in the world around you? Read on to find out!

Don't Ignore It!

Diversity is the state of having many people who are different from one another. When we respect diversity, we respect the fact that everyone is **unique** instead of ignoring our differences, or pretending they don't exist.

Treating everyone equally is an important part of respecting diversity. Some people believe the only way to treat everyone equally is to pretend everyone is exactly the same. However, this way of thinking ignores diversity. It's possible to treat everyone equally while still celebrating the things that make us different.

Facing the Facts 🔍

According to the United States Census Bureau, which studies the U.S. population, racial and ethnic diversity is growing in the United States. In 2016, it reported that the population of babies of a race other than white was larger than the population of white babies under one year old.

What's the word?

What does it mean?

ethnicity	a group of people who often come from the same place and share a common culture, or way of life
gender	the state of seeing yourself as male or female
race	a group of people who look alike in certain ways
religion	a belief system, often the belief in one or more gods

These are some of the different ways to look at diversity. People of different ethnicities, genders, races, and religions help make the United States such a diverse country. It's important to learn about what makes people different instead of ignoring those differences.

Coming from Different Countries

Ethnic diversity is an important part of diversity around the world, but it's especially important in the United States. This is because many people who live in the United States came from different countries or have family members who came from different countries many years ago. These **immigrants** brought their language, their culture, and even their favorite foods with them to their new home.

Many cities across the United States have **festivals** and parades every year to celebrate different ethnic groups. These events are a great way to learn about diverse cultures!

Facing the Facts

A 2016 study showed that Americans are more likely than Europeans to see cultural diversity as a good thing.

8

Some Americans don't support immigrants because they're afraid of people who come from other countries. However, most Americans like living in a country with a lot of ethnic diversity, and they want immigrants to feel welcome in the United States.

AMERICA'S GOT ROOM IMMIGRANTS WELCOME

Fighting Against Racism

When people come from different places, they often look different. In the United States, people of many different races live together. The fight to respect racial diversity in this country has been going on for hundreds of years.

Racism is still a part of life for many Americans. This is a system in which people are treated poorly because of their race. In the United States, white Americans have often been treated better than people of other races. However, many people are working to make sure people of all races are treated equally.

Facing the Facts 🔍

As of 2017, 58 percent of Americans saw racism as a major problem in their country.

Many Americans have parents of different races. This has made the United States an even more diverse country.

Women and the Workplace

Gender also plays an important part in diversity. This is especially true in the workplace. At many companies, the highest positions are all held by men. This lack of diversity means different points of view aren't always heard. By including more women in leadership **roles**, companies can create a more diverse working **environment**. This can lead to exciting new ideas.

A truly diverse workplace features people of different races and genders working together and being treated fairly. As of 2017, less than 50 percent of women believed the company they worked for was doing enough to make this happen.

Facing the Facts 🔍

In a 2017 study, 32 percent of women and 45 percent of men said they felt the company they worked for made diverse ideas a part of the decision-making **process**.

In the United States, many people believe there should be more diversity in certain fields of work, including business and science. One way to create a more diverse work environment is to make sure there's equal pay for equal work.

Diverse Points of View

Many people support diverse workplaces, schools, and communities because they believe it's good to be around different ways of thinking. In the United States, people are free to share many diverse points of view. When people share diverse beliefs respectfully, it helps others learn.

Respect is also an important part of dealing with diverse families and **relationships**. Every family is different. Some have a mom and a dad, while others have two moms or two dads. Other families might only have one parent or have guardians instead of parents.

Facing the Facts

Respecting diversity also means respecting people with disabilities. One way this happens is through inclusive education, which brings students with disabilities and students without disabilities into the same classroom to learn together.

People are becoming more accepting of different kinds of families. They know what matters most is how much love there is in a family—not what a family looks like.

Afraid of What's Different

Some people aren't respectful when **interacting** with others who are different from them. These people don't like diversity and often say or do unkind things toward people they see as different.

Intolerant people—people who aren't accepting of others' differences—are often afraid. They're often part of groups that have been in positions of power for a long time. They see a more diverse world as a world where they're powerless instead of a world where power is shared more equally. They want everyone to be like them, which is why they don't like to celebrate diversity.

Facing the Facts 🔍

Intolerant people often show prejudice toward people who are different from them. Prejudice is a bad feeling about someone that's not based in facts and is formed without getting to know that person.

Many people have gathered together to speak out against intolerance and in favor of diversity at marches in the United States and around the world.

Diversity Matters!

In the past, diversity wasn't always treated as an important issue. Today, however, more people are beginning to speak out about why diversity matters. For example, people are fighting for more diverse leadership in government. They believe having more female leaders and leaders of different races will help governments better **represent** all the people they serve.

People are also fighting for more diversity in movies and on television. When movies and television shows are made by many different kinds of people, different stories are told. These stories can **inspire** everyone instead of just one group of people.

Facing the Facts 🔍

Between 2007 and 2016, 4.2 percent of movie directors and 31.4 percent of the characters who spoke in movies were women.

Diversity in movies and on television shows is important because it helps people understand that different groups of people all have important stories to tell. The success of movies such as *Wonder Woman* and *Black Panther* showed that people like seeing more diversity on the big screen.

A Challenge or a Chance to Learn?

Diversity is a part of life. We meet people from different places, people who look different from us, and people who think differently than we do every day. Some people might see this as a **challenge**, but many people see it as a chance to learn more about the world.

Sometimes differences can seem scary, but diversity is nothing to be afraid of. In fact, it's something to celebrate! Talking about the importance of diversity can help more people feel accepted in the world around them. This helps build a world where everyone feels welcome—no matter how different they may seem.

Facing the Facts

In a 2017 study, 64 percent of Americans said they believe racial and ethnic diversity makes the United States a better country.

WHAT CAN YOU DO?

Learn more about different ethnicities, races, and other groups of people.

Talk and listen respectfully to people who are different from you.

Visit a festival or a parade that celebrates another culture.

Tell an adult if you see someone being picked on for being different.

Talk openly about why you feel diversity is important.

Watch movies and television shows that tell diverse stories.

Think about the different things that make you special.

It's good to be different! These are just some of the ways you can celebrate diversity and show all people acceptance and respect.

GLOSSARY

challenge: A problem.

environment: Everything that is around a person.

festival: A time or event set aside to celebrate.

immigrant: A person who comes to a country to live there.

inspire: To move someone to do something great.

interact: To come together and have an effect on each other.

process: A set of actions.

relationship: The way in which two or more people are connected.

represent: To act officially or stand for someone or something.

role: A part, job, or function.

unique: Special or different from anything else.

FOR MORE INFORMATION

WEBSITES

Teaching Tolerance: Mix It Up

www.tolerance.org/mix-it-up

This is the official website of Mix It Up at Lunch Day, which calls for students to sit with different people at lunch one day each year to learn more about diversity in their school.

"What Is Diversity?"

www.cyh.com/HealthTopics/HealthTopicDetailsKids.aspx?p=335&np=286&id=2345

This article helps readers better understand the different ways diversity can be found in the world around them and the reasons why some people aren't accepting of diversity.

BOOKS

Colby, Jennifer. *Stories of Diversity.* Ann Arbor, MI: Cherry Lake Publishing, 2018.

Ogden, Charlie. *Equality and Diversity.* New York, NY: Crabtree Publishing Company, 2017.

Suen, Anastasia. *Respecting Diversity.* Vero Beach, FL: Rourke Educational Media, 2014.

INDEX